I0469470

This Book is for You Stupid

Stupid Mistakes That Cost You Sales

Written by Mathew Koenig

Copyright Info

This Book is for You Stupid
Published by KonigCo LLC
2920 Business One Dr.
Suite 113
Kalamazoo, MI 49048

www.konig.co

Dedication

To my children. This book is yet another example of my nagging comment to you: "Everything that you do is a choice that has consequences that are either positive or negative so remember that every decision you make in your life is important." Every decision I've made in business has been with the goal of providing you with a better life.

Preface

If you're looking for a grammatically well-written book by someone with an MBA that will put you to sleep; this is the wrong book for you. *However*, if you're looking for a book written by someone who has spent 20 years in the trenches of sales, succeeding AND failing over and over so that you can learn from their efforts and improve your career....READ THIS BOOK!

The late, great, Zig Ziglar once said: "You can get anything you want in life if you are just willing to help enough other people get what they want."

Those words have been a constant inspiration in my sales career so *I want* to help you get what *you want*. That said, I believe that everyone who gets into sales really *wants* to be successful but most of them, like me, start out with little or no direction, knowledge or training on *how* to reach that goal of success.

This means that we start out "stupid" in our sales career. When we don't know what we're doing, we look for advice from our peers but unfortunately they have little more training than we do, they've just got the experience of 'time served' so technically, they're "stupid" too.

I'm not saying it to be mean because it's not totally their fault, their manager was probably "stupid" too and his manager probably was too.

In sales, too many of us have learned from those who did their best but really didn't have the knowledge, talent, or ability to give us what we needed to be successful so the stupid cycle just keeps going.

This book will show you how to completely F*$K up your sales career. Hopefully this book will put a few smiles on your face while sharing real life examples of epic sales failures as well as solid practices for how to 'Stop the Stupid'.

Table of Contents

For more information on creating an active table of contents using Microsoft Word, go here:
http://support.microsoft.com/kb/285059

Chapter 1: Stupid Liars

"Don't let them turn you into a liar." – Alyce Lou Isom, 1929-1994

I had just been hired at the local Chevrolet Dealership in South Haven, Michigan when I was 17 years old and the General Manager, Sam, told me that I could make around $50,000 dollars which seemed HUGE to me at that time so I was excited.

Alyce Lou Isom was my Grandmother and one of the most wonderful women in the entire world. She loved everybody and rarely had a negative thing to say. From my early teen years on, I lived most of my life with her so she was a major influence in my life and more of a Mom than a Grandmother.

I had just been fired from my job at an office supply store downtown and I was freaking out because at 17, I had a child on the way. Yes, I know, babies having babies right? What can I say…we all know how babies are made and it's fun.

Anyway, my Dad called his buddy who was the Finance Manager at this Chevy store and he got me an interview with Sam. When I got hired I couldn't believe it! I was sure that a ton of other people wanted this job but at 17 years old, he actually saw something in this chubby kid from South Haven, that lead him to think that I was better than all of the other people who applied. Sam saw something in me that told him I was destined to be a success.

"You start on Monday kid. Get here at 8AM and don't' be late."

I was so excited that I had to tell my Grandma immediately. Back then we didn't have cell phones though because I was super poor so I had to wait until I got back to my apartment. When I called her and told her the good news she said: "Don't let them turn you into a liar."

If you've read my first book, Winners & Losers, you've heard this story already so I'm sorry if you're reading it again but it's important for this book.

See, I didn't really get what she meant by that remark. All salespeople aren't liars are they?

Monday morning when I got to work I found out that I was just one out of 5 salespeople hired at the store and I later learned that this was common for dealers back then. They'd hire four or five salespeople at a time, throwing them out there to sell and seeing which ones would

"stick".
This genius idea comes from the idea of taking spaghetti noodles and throwing them against the wall. If they stick, they're done, if they fall off, they're not ready.

Stupid right? What that dealer didn't know back then was that with a little training, I could have been the best salesperson that they'd ever hired. I was young, eager, fairly smart, and willing to do whatever it took to serve the customer better than anyone else. The problem was: I didn't know how.

The bigger problem was: They didn't know how to serve the customer so how could they possibly help me become successful? $50,000 at 17 years old wasn't even a remote possibility at that dealership for an inexperienced untrained salesperson like myself.

Now I understood what my Grandmother meant about them being "liars" and I knew that I didn't want to be thought of in the same light as the people that hired me.

When I was hired, I wasn't given an honest expectation of what each day would look like. I wasn't given any training on how to greet customers, how to ask quality questions, how to listen to the wants and needs of the buyer, how to demonstrate to those wants and needs or how to ask for the sale. I was given a desk and a phone book and an ashtray (because everyone smoked back then apparently) and I was given a stack of brochures.

Let's fast forward time a few years. When working as a sales manager for the first time I was able to grow my department by 67% in profit and 42% in unit sales during the first eighteen months in that role. My department, which was a less than popular franchise at the time, grew more than any other franchise in our automotive group.

When I went to work for my first dot com, I took a market which had failed for 10 years under the guidance of an affiliate, and made that territory the number one direct territory for growth in just 10 months.

As a sales training manager for that same dot com, I had the privilege of working with some of the best minds in the country to create and implement sales strategies that would change online automotive advertising forever.

While working for my next dot com I had the honor of helping launch their first ever direct to dealer program. My efforts, and resulting success, lead that company to a commitment that would shift their entire business model just nine months later. This shift added millions of dollars in revenue, quadrupled their sales staff and has lead them to develop new products and services that help their clients and end user consumers have a better experience overall.

I'm not telling you any of this as a pat on the back for myself because my accomplishments are nothing compared to others out there. Heck, I have friends and business associates that have accomplished tenfold what I've done and I look at them as phenomenal people that I continue to learn from.

I'm sharing with this you to show you how stupid the thinking at my first dealership was. I was just a silly wide-eyed teenager to that first fella who hired me. I was just another salesman that didn't 'stick' but had they been honest with me about what to expect, and what effort was required; I could have been a success. Instead, they lied about how easy it would be and expected enthusiasm & natural talent to be enough.

The reason I had success at other Auto Groups, the reason I was fortunate enough to experience success with companies like Cars.com and Edmunds.com was because I was surrounded by professionals that were committed to helping me *learn to better myself* so that I could better those around me.

Cars.com has an amazing team of leaders like Dennis, Alex, John, Hans and Ralph who were willing to call me out and put my ego in check (which was needed often) so that I could open myself up to glean from their expertise. As a result, I was able to learn more about serving the people on our sales team instead of focusing on serving myself. That great leadership at Cars.com is why their product, and their team, are some of the best in the business.

At Edmunds.com I had the pleasure of learning from Johnny G who is one of the most talented and outgoing sales professionals in the Automotive Industry. John's experience in the Financial Sector and Automotive Sector were second to none and he gave me tools and constant motivation and education so that I could better myself, which in turn helped our clients and their clients.

Both Cars.com and Edmunds.com set honest expectations, they helped create honest goals, and they were honest with me about what I needed to do in order to improve myself, and improve the overall company.

These companies were, and still are, very *smart* in their assimilation process and their ongoing training.

Because of their honest approach, I was able to learn from both of these companies and put many of those best practices to use for my clients.

Unfortunately for that first dealership that hired me, their methods lead them to go out of business just a few short years after I worked there. I guess there weren't enough people who 'stuck'.

Get Smart Challenge: What is one stupid habit or method of thinking that you need to get rid of in order to move forward in your career?

Chapter 2: Stupid Kids

Today we have stupid adults because we are training our children to be stupid. I can already hear a few of you crybabies saying, "whoa my child is far from stupid, he is a straight A student and he is in accelerated reading and math etc.,…"

SO WHAT! I don't mean they are uneducated in the realm of academics, I mean that you're making them stupid in the ways of the world.

Let me make it easy to understand.

In life, you either WIN or you LOSE. There is no middle ground, no tie, and no draw. Win or Lose. You get the sale or you don't. You get the job or you don't. You get the girl or you don't. You get the championship ring or you don't. You WIN or you LOSE.

What does this have to do with our kids? We set stupid expectations with them for life from the time that they're playing team sports like little league and flag football. Listen, I'm not saying that the one kid who wins the spelling bee is a winner and the other 40 kids who didn't win are losers. I'm saying that we set a false expectation for kids when we say "It doesn't matter if you win or lose."

That saying is complete hogwash! It matters if you win. Winning sets the stage for other great things. Losing can also be a great motivator. If we handle losing well with our kids, it can lead them to experience many other 'wins' going forward and sometimes that loss on the field can be a teachable moment with our children and those teachable moments are small victories too.

I'll give you an example of how this works in real life with my own son. I have an eleven year old named Liam (he's 11 right now as I write this book) and the kid is a rock star athlete in the making. From the time he was young he had natural talent in football, basketball and baseball. Since Liam has been fortunate enough to experience natural talent, when he was younger he had a very hard time if he experienced any moments of failure. I remember one game in particular where our team, the Chargers, was facing the Packers. The Packers were experienced and their coach was a touch ex-detective who worked in an undercover narcotics unit for years and he ran his program like a boot camp.

My son was our quarterback and no matter how hard he tried, he couldn't make a play that day because the other team was just flat out better at football. Just before half-time Liam threw an incomplete pass and he was so mad that he actually put himself on the bench. Yes, he benched himself at six years old. He walked to the sideline, took off his Jersey and said "Dad I stink, put someone else in there because I can't go back on the field."

At this point some other kid's mom said "Liam you're doing fine out there honey, you don't stink." And as his dad, believe me I wanted to say the same thing because I love him but what would that teach him? It's ok to give up, you're great, you're awesome.

I know he's awesome and I know he's great and I knew at that time, he would grow up to be an amazing athlete but I also knew that his future would depend on each and every one of these teachable moments so I called a time out and handled it this way:

"Liam, you're *not* doing fine out there. I love you, and I know you're good but you're right, you're getting crushed and every time you have a tough play you're getting worse because you're getting mad and letting that goof you up. I *won't let you quit just because you're not doing good. If you quit now, you'll always be a quitter and I love you too much to let you quit. Your team needs you and they need you to try your best so put your jersey back on and get out there NOW and show them that just because you messed up doesn't mean it's over. Plus, if you don't go out there and give it your all, you're going to be grounded from video games because I'm not rewarding you for quitting."*

Super mean right? Think again. He went out there, threw pass after pass and we kicked the Packers ass after that little speech!

Pause: I'm kidding, he didn't.

What really happened? He went back out there, tried his hardest, our team made a few good plays to get on the board once or twice and we still got our asses handed to us.

At the end of the game, almost every kid on our team was crying as all of the parents made a tunnel and cheered for our boys (and the one girl on our team) while they ran through it.

Crying kids means they didn't have fun right? *Wrong!* They had fun playing but they were all disappointed by the loss. These kids had a burning desire to win and I never squashed that. I didn't lie to the kids and say, "it doesn't matter if you win or lose" because they deserve the truth.

Kids are smart and they know when we try to feed them bullshit. When you say, "it doesn't matter if you win or lose", you're telling them: "I don't care how you feel about winning or losing."

The reality is that it matters to the kid just like it matters to you and I today. It hurts to lose and it's ok to learn that at a young age because it helps us try even harder NOT to lose when we

get older. Losing sucks but when we lose, we
can learn from those losses.

Chapter 3: Stupid Managers

Few things are worse for an organization than stupid managers. Every team needs a leader to guide them in the right direction. Unfortunately in many sales organizations, there are more managers than there are leaders.

Let's look at the definition for both from Dictionary.com:

Leader – a person or thing that leads. A guiding or directing head, as of an army, movement, or political group.

Manager – a person who has control or direction of an institution, business, etc., or of a part, division or phase of it. A person who controls and manipulates resources and expenditures, as of a household.

After a quick glance at these two definitions do you see a glaring problem with Managers?

Leaders "guide" and "direct" but Managers *"control" and "manipulate"*.

Do you like being controlled or manipulated? Of course you don't, and neither does anyone else!

For a sales organization, the people on your sales team are your most valuable 'resources' and great sales people are looking for quality Leaders to help them grow in their career. Great sales people are looking for quality Leaders to help them improve their selling skills, their communication skills, and often times they're looking for someone who can help them grow into a role as a great LEADER.

Sadly, many organizations have managers at the help who spend their time looking for ways to control their 'resources' by 'manipulating' them with intimidation, constant changes in compensation, and promises of promotion.

What these stupid Managers don't realize is that their sales people, the good ones at least, won't tolerate the manipulation for very long before they're out hunting for a better work environment. These stupid managers don't realize that their sales people are willing to be lead; even if that means they'll be lead away to a competing company.

Chapter 4: Stupid Ads

This chapter is touchy because there are differences in each market, however, there are some common sense bits of advertising stupidity that transcend market and demographics so let's talk about these stupid ads.

Stupid Ad Tactic #1: Advertising "Everyone's Approved"

No matter where you live, you've seen the dealership that advertises that "Good Credit, Bad Credit, Everybody Drives" type of promotion right? Who do you think that ad will attract?

Duh! It's targeted to folks with credit challenges right? The reason this Ad is stupid is that it actually works.

Right now you're thinking: "The author of this book must be stupid, he just said that the Ad is stupid because it works."

Stay with me here reader. When this Ad works, it brings in that large group of people that most of the dealers are unable to provide financing for. Sure the Ad says "everybody is approved" but really the dealer is hoping that they'll get a lot of folks coming in and that a good portion of those people will actually have better credit than they realize.

Unfortunately, what happens with this situation is that out of the 100 people that come in, only about 5 or 10 of those folks are able to get approved and come up with the co-signer or down payment necessary to get a vehicle.

That means that the other 90-95 people who came in will leave disappointed and feeling like the dealer's ads were false. What's even WORSE is that the sales people in many cases will end up pre-qualifying all of the customers who come in during these 'bad credit' sales and that means that the 'good credit' customers get a shitty experience too and they will typically leave because they don't have to tolerate that pre-qualifying experience.

Side note: People with bad credit are still PEOPLE and they deserve to be treated with respect too!

Unfortunately, the ad asks for people with bad credit to come in, then the sales people are pissed off when they find out that almost everyone they deal with during the sale has bad credit so they treat people poorly, their overall morale goes in the toilet, and the dealership is actually doing more damage than good.

On top of losing good credit buyers due to the

stupid treatment from the stupid ad, let's think about the bad credit buyers for a moment…the ones that couldn't buy a car because their credit wasn't quite up to par yet. When their credit is better, do you actually think they'll ever go back to that dealership?

If you said: "probably not", you're probably right. Instead, they'll tell all their friends that the dealer advertises things that it can't deliver on and they'll look for other options when they're finally in a position to buy a vehicle.

Stupid Ad Tactic #2: Free $20 Gift Card with a Test Drive

Incentives are attractive for customers and I know that some dealers right now are saying "we run that promotion and sell a lot of vehicles from it" but I'm going to ask you to set your ego aside for a moment and consider using some common sense.

Would you spend $20,000 on a vehicle just because you got a $20 gift card to Chili's or Best Buy?

Since I know that everyone who is intelligent just said "no", I'm going to ask you another common sense question:

Do you honestly think that your customers are that much stupider than you are?

Hopefully you said "no" to that question too.

Don't be stupid! If someone came in with one of those 'gift card' test drive slips it is for one of two reasons:

Reason #1 (Least likely but possible) They aren't in the market for a car but they're so down on their luck that they'll waste an hour of your time driving your new car and getting paid $20 to do it.

Reason #2 (The most likely reason) They were already interested in your vehicles and planning to come to your dealership anyway. If you don't believe me I'd encourage you to consider the following things.

Where did they see your little gift card promotion? Typically that's something from a pop-up on your website.

Why were they at your website instead of Cars.com, Edmunds.com or Autotrader.com? Oh that's right...it's because they're already very interested in your product!

Stop being stupid with your advertising! Effective advertising will always accomplish one of two goals. It will either help you keep customers that you already have or it will help you win new customers that you did not already have.

At the end of the day, those are your two goals. I'm going to insert a shameless plug here because I know how to accomplish those two goals.

My company, KonigCo (www.konig.co) offers mobile marketing products that help my clients get & keep customers. We use SMS technology to deliver incentives to customers who *buy* from our clients. Yes…customers who BUY.

Instead of offering someone $20 to drive your car, and then negotiating money off of your car, offer them $200 off of the purchase of your vehicle. This way, you're giving a consumer a financial benefit to BUY from you instead of $20 to consider you.

I'm sorry but if it comes down to you or my local dealer, I'm not driving to your place for some lame-ass $20 gift card.

My Dealer clients have powerful CTAs (Calls to Action) on all of their Ads like their Cars.com leaderboards & power position ads. They use CTAs on their Facebook Ad Campaigns to generate real ROI instead of 'likes' on their page. My Dealers have photos and overlays that say things like "Get additional savings on this vehicle, text SALES to 71441".

When a customer sends the word "SALES" to

the phone number 71441, they instantly receive a coupon from the Dealership that has their offer. Usually the offer is something like '$200 off any vehicle in stock' but the best part is that **my clients instantly get an email and text message with the consumer's mobile phone number so they can call the buyer and say "I wanted to make sure you receive the incentive offer, by the way, when would you like to stop in and take that Camry for a test drive?"**

I know that this section had a few paragraphs promoting my business but I know that my business delivers common sense strategy to my clients so I'd be stupid if I didn't share every opportunity I know of to help you get better.

You don't have to do business with me, but if you're not using CTAs in EVERY advertisement that you have, you're missing opportunities to sell more product and make more money so Ads without a Call to Action that can convert lookers into buyers are STUPID ADS and let's face it, smart people shouldn't run stupid ads.

Chapter 5: Stupid Customer Service

Today is the perfect day to write this chapter because I have had the week of Customer Service HELL with a few MAJOR companies and guess what, I'm going to share those shitty experiences with you in this chapter.

Stupid Customer Service Company #1: Verizon Wireless

Recently I opened an account with Verizon Wireless for our family. Our account has 7 lines (we have 5 kiddos) and our bill is $500 per month. When we opened the account my wife tried a different phone than she'd ever had before and unfortunately the phone was a turd. It was an HTC Rezound and it overheated and the battery only lasted about 3 hours. After using the phone for a week she wanted to exchange it. We called Verizon and the guy on the phone was great. He even said: "You guys just opened up 7 lines with us so I'm going to talk to my boss and get the re-stocking fee waived for you with this return." Unfortunately, the phone my wife wanted wasn't available for pre-order yet so we had to wait three days to get her phone ordered. No big deal right? WRONG!

Three days later, I called Verizon and the new

rep I spoke to had nothing noted on the account from the previous conversation and she said there was no way she could waive the re-stocking fee.

Note: I would have been happy to pay the stupid fee but since the other guy suggested that they would waive it, I now had an expectation of it being waived so this became a matter of principal.

She put me on hold and spoke to her manager and said "since there are no notes in the system, there's no way for us to know that our rep really promised to waive the fee for you."

Translated: "Mr. Koenig we think you're lying to try and screw us out of $35."

Really? I have seven lines of service and a $500 monthly bill but I'm really trying to screw them out of $35? Are they really that stupid?

In a word: YES.

I asked for her 'manager' since she didn't have the authority to waive it. Her manager called me back only to say the EXACT SAME THING! Basically Verizon said that they couldn't risk the $35 because the representative hadn't put notes in the system and if they honored it based on my word, they'd have to honor it for anyone else who says a rep told them something.

Here is why Verizon is STUPID. I was only 10 days into the agreement with Verizon wireless, which means I still had 20 days to CANCEL COMPLETELY and shift over to another carrier.

Verizon was willing to throw away $12,000 ($500/mo. x 24 months of contract) in order to save $35. Their stupid customer service attitude not only turns us away as customers but this experience is being shared with you, and every other ready of this book, and all of my Twitter followers. Stupid move Verizon, Stupid move.

Stupid Customer Service Company #2: Cisco

Today I called Cisco because the router I purchased from them 6 months ago was having issues. The Wi-Fi signal was randomly dropping and it wouldn't transmit a signal at all when connecting an Ethernet cable.

I tested it, reset it, etc., and the router had a physical flaw that needed to be replaced. When I called them and explained exactly what it was doing, the stupid rep asked me to plug the cable directly into my laptop Ethernet port.

I did, even though I explained that their outgoing port wasn't working, and surprise…it wouldn't connect. After 30 minutes of trouble shooting the girl with broken English wanted me to try doing another 20 minutes worth of ideas.

Instead, I threw the router in the garbage, went to a much more expensive Apple Time Capsule Router and made the decision to never deal with Cisco again because their customer service reps don't listen to their customers and treat them like they're stupid instead.

Stupid Customer Service Company #3: Dell

Recently I ordered a macked out laptop from Dell to use for work. NOTE: I'm not typically a Windows fan but I gave it a shot because I had a great experience with Dell about seven years ago. The ordering process was great, shipping was great and the laptop was great for the first 48 days. Then the Wi-Fi card began sporadically telling the laptop that it didn't exist and the screen began flickering as if it had an electrical short.

When buying this laptop, I also paid a little extra for the upgraded coverage from Dell. When I called them to explain the issues, they offered to send a technician from a computer repair shop close by, to come and 'repair' the issues.

Repair the issues? It's barely over a month old and over $1,000 and they want to send little Timmy from the Geek Squad to come to my home or business and tear it apart and try to fix it with whatever parts they have in stock at his repair shop?

I let them know that this solution was stupid. I told the representative from Dell that they needed to just replace it instead of hacking up my brand new laptop. The rep on the phone said that he didn't have the authority to do that.

He then had his manager call me back (which I'm sure wasn't cheap since they're a call center overseas) only to tell me that even though he is the manager, he has no authority to replace the laptop either.

Now we see where the service rep learned his stupid customers service skills.

At the end of the call the manager scheduled an appointment for someone from their corporate office to call me for resolution on the situation. I guess we'll see what the resolution is for the situation in three days (note: I'll be sure to put it in the book).

What was it that caused each of these companies to lose a customer and end up looking stupid to thousands of readers and thousands of people that are connected to me online?

None of these companies have empowered their employees to serve their customers. Successful businesses empower their employees to take care of the people who are spending money with them. If you're going to be stupid, be overtly stupid with how overboard you go to make your customer happy instead of seeing what you can get away with before *losing* a customer for life.

So many companies spend thousands of dollars on advertising campaigns to let people know how great their customer service is yet their great customer service is only coming from the sales people who have to be friendly to earn a commission.

Stupid companies like Dell and Verizon need to stop spending money on ads and professional photos that paint a picture of great employees providing great customer service and instead they should shift those dollars into a customer satisfaction fund or a training program for their employees.

Good business is about getting and *keeping* customers and poor customer service is STUPID because it's losing current customers and costing you potential sales their friends and family members.

Companies are allowed to make mistakes and products are allowed to fail. How the company handles these issues will determine whether they're viewed as great or stupid.

Chapter 6: Stupid Sales People

On the topic of getting customers, we have to turn the spotlight on our most valuable resource: Sales People.

Stop for a moment and think about a terrible experience that you've had when trying to purchase something. (This exercise won't be hard for most people.)

What made that experience a bad one? What did the sales person do that was stupid?

Usually a poor sales experience has multiple stupid moments and they start with a lack of listening on the part of the sales person. When they don't listen, they end up showing you a product that doesn't fit your wants and needs. When they realize that you're not excited about the product they show you, they'll either drop the price, which costs their company profit, or they start being pushy, which causes customers to leave and ultimately costs the company profit.

Why do companies keep allowing their sales people to be stupid? Let's think of this in relation to my favorite business, the Automotive Industry. Oh, before you think I'm picking on Car Dealers I want to clearly tell you that I am not picking on them at all. I reference them often because my entire career since I have been seventeen years of age has been in the Automotive Industry.

Back to the action…

In the dealership, there are some great sales training companies like the Cardone Group and the Verde Group. With either one of these companies, a dealership can spend around $1,500 to train their sales person on the basics of serving a customer properly.

Unfortunately, most dealers skip over this valuable training and allow their sales people to practice their skills on the customer instead.

Let's say that the average sales person will talk to 50 customers per month. That average sales person sells a car to 10 of those customers with an average profit of $2,000 per vehicle sold.

This means that 40 customers left and took their $2,000 of profit per vehicle with them so the dealership loses $80,000 of potential profit. Multiply that x 12 months and the dealership could be losing $960,000 of potential profit in a year.

Now multiply that x 10 sales people and we're talking about losing $9.6 MILLION DOLLARS BECAUSE WE DIDN'T SPEND $1,500 per person to train our sales people properly.

It doesn't take a math major to realize that it's stupid to let our sales people practice on our customers.

Smart companies realize that it's important to train their sales people in a way that will help them learn to listen to the customer's wants, needs and desires.

Smart companies realize that it's important to train their sales people on how to give a customer focused presentation and demonstration of their products.

Smart companies realize that it's important to train their sales people on how to understand why potential buyers object so that they can learn to handle those objections the right way.

Smart companies realize that training is not an option and that their sales team needs to be equipped to handle the wants and needs of their consumers.

Basically, if you're not training your sales people, they're going to end up making stupid mistakes that cost your company a ridiculous amount of money.

Chapter 7: Stupid Habits

Everyone of us have habits that are sure to annoy the hell out of someone else but some habits are worse than others. Let's take a quick peek at some of the stupid habits that cost sales people money.

Stupid Habit #1: Smoking

-   If you're a smoker, and you're smoking at work, you're stupid. Nearly every state in the union has made it obvious that smokers aren't welcome. Sure, it's your right to be a smoker but what you may not realize is that your smoking is costing you money at work! I'm not just talking about the expense of your cigarettes or your health care costs because frankly, I don't care about your lungs if you don't. A fact that you can't argue is that people who smoke have an odor that cannot be covered by cologne or air freshener. This means your potential customers who *aren't* smokers probably think you stink. If they think you stink, they don't want to be in a car with you on a test drive, let alone your office with the door closed. If you are a smoker, keep your smelly habit for after work because losing sales over your smelly habit is just plain stupid.

Stupid Habit #2: The Circle of Stupid

- When you're in sales, you need to have a positive attitude. Unfortunately, certain events at work or in your personal life may have some ups and downs that put you in a crummy mood. We all have a bad day here and there but one sure fire way to ruin your day is to spend time in the circle of stupid. What's the circle of stupid? It's that group of sales people standing around complaining about the inventory, the manager's appraisals, the economy, the weather, the president, or the results of American Idol. Standing around sharing negative stories is just flat stupid and when you see that circle, run away fast because that circle of stupid will cost you sales every time.

Stupid Habit #3: Waiting for Customers

- It seems that today's sales person has forgotten the importance of prospecting for business. Walk in to any dealership today and 75% of the sales people are sitting on their ass waiting for customers to come to them. Did you know there is a goldmine of customers in the service department? Did you know that you have a database of customers who have friends and family members who will be buying vehicles in the future at some point? Stop waiting for customers to come to you and pick up your phone to reach out to them instead. Waiting for opportunity is stupid.

Chapter 8: Stupid Advice

Thanks to the Internet, everyone has become a so-called "expert" in his or her field. Go to any Automotive Conference and you'll find experts in everything from Google Adwords to Social Media Marketing and they're all eager to give you advice on how to run your dealership.

Expert #1 has a new YouTube video every other day so he must know how to run an Internet department.

Expert #2 writes a new blog post about your industry each day so she must be the best of the best when it comes to blogging.

Expert #3 does a webinar each month so he must be an expert at whatever he is talking about and he also has three or four other 'experts' that say he's an expert so obviously it's true.

If someone hasn't spent a considerable amount of time in your store, and your market, how can they tell you that you're doing something wrong?

Sure there are some common sense basics that transcend market, etc., but you don't need an 'expert' to give you that advice do you? Heck no, you just need to pull your head out of your ass and do the right things:

- Put your customers first
- Empower your sales team to serve the customer
- Pay attention to the competitors and find a way to dominate your space
- Differentiate yourself from the others in your market
- Listen better than anyone else that you compete with
- Keep your place of business clean and professional
- Invest in quality training for your staff
- Be consistent with your message
- Stop advertising to bad credit and complaining when that's what you get
- Stop assuming the guy on YouTube knows how to run a BDC just because he knows how to turn on a webcam
- Stop listening to stupid advice from people who don't know you or your business
- Don't assume that I know what I'm talking about if it doesn't make sense

If you're always focused on the two things that keep your business moving forward, Getting & Keeping Customers, you'll be able to weed out the stupid advice.

Chapter 9: Don't Stay Stupid

Hopefully you've had some fun with this book and picked up some common sense strategies at the same time.

If you got anything from this book I hope that you grasped the importance of using common sense to improve your business in these times where your competition keeps doing the same stupid things over and over again.

There is nobody else on the planet that knows your business better than you, but you can only continue to improve the business if you continue improving yourself.

John Wooden said: "Be observing constantly. Stay open minded. Be eager to **learn** and improve."

Keep your eyes open for great ideas. Keep your mind open to try new things that seem to make sense. Most of all, *always stay hungry and push to better yourself each and every day so you don't stay stupid!*

Now go out there and make today amazing!

Resource Page

About the Author:

Mat Koenig is an Author and Professional Speaker with 20 years of experience in professional sales and sales training. Mat has served at world-renowned companies such as Edmunds.com and Cars.com helping increase sales and profit.

Mat is the founder and CEO of KonigCo in Kalamazoo, MI, which is dedicated to helping Automotive Dealers, and Small business owners reach consumers using mobile marketing.

He is married with three children, and two stepchildren and lives in Western Michigan.

Learn more about KonigCo by visiting.....
http://www.konig.co